FASLANE

Jenna Watt

FASLANE

in association with Showroom and Contact

OBERON BOOKS
LONDON
WWW.OBERONBOOKS.COM

First published in 2017 by Oberon Books Ltd
521 Caledonian Road, London N7 9RH
Tel: +44 (0) 20 7607 3637 / Fax: +44 (0) 20 7607 3629
e-mail: info@oberonbooks.com
www.oberonbooks.com

A catalogue record for this book is available from the British Library.

PB ISBN: 9781786821072
E ISBN: 9781786821089

Cover photo by Mihaela Bodlovic

"An extraordinary piece of documentary theatre."
★ ★ ★ ★ ★ British Theatre Guide

Faslane previewed at Contact's Flying Solo Festival in May 2016 and premiered at the Edinburgh Fringe 2016 at Summerhall receiving a Scotsman Fringe First Award and an inaugural Summerhall Lustrum Award.

It first toured in Spring 2017 to:
EASTERHOUSE Platform, COVE Cove Burgh Hall, INVERNESS Eden Court, BUCKIE Royal British Legion Hall, FORT WILLIAM Caol Community Centre, ISLE OF MULL Comar, DUMFRIES Swallow Theatre, GLASGOW Tron Theatre, BANCHORY Woodend Barn, FINDHORN Universal Hall, LEEDS West Yorkshire Playhouse, EDINBURGH Summerhall, DUNDEE Dundee Rep, STIRLING Macrobert Arts Centre, TARLAND MacRobert Memorial Hall, GIFFNOCK Eastwood Park Theatre, LONDON Camden People's Theatre and UMEÅ (Sweden) Teaterförening.

Faslane is a Contact Flying Solo Commission.

Faslane was supported in development by:
Creative Scotland Artist's Bursaries, Contact, Cove Park, A National Theatre of Scotland Artist Attachment & West Yorkshire Playhouse.

ALBA | CHRUTHACHAIL

CREATIVE TEAM
Written and Performed by Jenna Watt
Produced by Callum Smith for Showroom
Sound Design by Kim Moore
Dramaturgy by Louise Stephens
Lighting Design by Alex Willy
Stage Manager Valentino Fabbreschi

www.jennawatt.co.uk

THANKS
Roxy Moores, Chris Thorpe, Matt Fenton, Nathan Keziyah, Caroline Newall, Anna Hodgart, Sam Phillips, Gilly Roche, Nick Bone, Christine Devaney, Harry Giles, Andrew Gibson, Sean Morris, Verity Leigh, David, Jane, Brian, Sam, Craig, Eric, Stewart Swan, John Lyndon, Mhari Robinson, Contact, West Yorkshire Playhouse, Battersea Arts Centre, Single End Collective, BaaD, Summerhall, Independencelive.net

SHOWROOM is an award-winning theatre company committed to working with the finest independent artists and small companies, providing producing support and organisational structure to those with none. The company's productions include Scottish tours of Jenna Watt's *Faslane* and *How You Gonna Live Your Dash*, New Room Theatre's *Blackout* and Sleeping Warrior's *The Rise and Inevitable Fall of Lucas Petit*. At the Edinburgh Fringe, the company has produced *Faslane* (Jenna Watt, Fringe First winner), *Denton and Me* (Sam Rowe, part of the Made in Scotland Showcase) and *Epic Love and Pop Song* by Phoebe Eclair-Powell.

www.weareshowroom.co.uk
@WeAreShowroom

Contact is the leading UK arts organisation to place young people's leadership and decision-making at the heart of everything. Young people aged 13-25 work alongside our staff to decide and deliver our artistic programme, and make staff and board appointments. Our vision is a world where young people are empowered by creativity to become leaders in the arts and in their own communities.

Contact commissions and produces up to 10 new shows each year for national touring, most with a focus on pressing social or ethical issues. Recent shows include *No Guts, No Heart, No Glory* (Common Wealth), *Rites* (with National Theatre Scotland), *The Spalding Suite* (with Southbank Centre and FUEL), *Big Girl's Blouse* (Kate O'Donnell), *Credible Likeable Superstar Role Model* (Bryony Kimmings), *The Shrine of Everyday Things* and *Under the Covers* (Contact Young Company).

Contact presents a pioneering year-round programme of theatre, dance, spoken word, music and comedy for all ages, alongside free weekly skills development activities and flagship young leadership programmes, including Future Fires (community arts leaders) and The Agency (young social entrepreneurs).

Contact is funded by Arts Council England, Manchester City Council, The Association of Greater Manchester Authorities and the University of Manchester.

'the most successful example of participatory decision-making in the arts' International Journal of Arts Management

'Manchester's most progressive theatre programme' Creative Tourist

Website: www.contactmcr.com
Twitter: @ContactMcr

Jenna Watt

(writer & performer)

Jenna Watt is an award-winning Scottish theatre maker. Her works include *Faslane*; winner of a Scotsman Fringe First and Summerhall Lustrum Award 2016 (Contact Manchester, Showroom), *How You Gonna Live Your Dash* (Showroom / Platform Easterhouse), Scotsman Fringe First award-winning *Flâneurs* (Summerhall, Battersea Arts Centre, Traverse Theatre, Tron Theatre, Woodend Barn, Mayfest, Play Pieces, Cumbernauld Theatre, Big Burns Supper), *Little Vikings are Never Lost* (The Arches, National Review of Live Art) and *It's OK, It's Only Temporary*; the apple smashing piece (Battersea Arts Centre, The Arches, Forest Fringe, Edinburgh Peer Group, The Basement).

Jenna has worked on projects for companies including; The National Theatre of Scotland, Traverse Theatre, Magnetic North, Unlimited Theatre, Northern Stage, Made In China, The Macrobert Young Company, Scottish Youth Theatre, Buzzcut Glasgow, The Arches, Forest Fringe, Junction 25, Lung Ha Theatre Company, National Review of Live Art, The Basement and the Arnolfini.

www.jennawatt.co.uk

Kim Moore (sound designer)

Kim Moore is a Glasgow-based composer and sound designer. She released two albums with Glasgow indie band Zoey Van Goey, and now works as a solo artist across a variety of platforms including theatre, dance and visual artists. In the past she has worked with Ankur productions, Eilidh MacAskill (Fish and Game), Lung Ha Theatre Company, Magnetic North, National Theatre of Scotland, NUX and Barrowland Ballet, and contemporary music establishments such as Scottish Music Centre and The City Halls. In 2013 she was awarded PRS Women Make Music Fund for a commission for an original live score for the 1936 film *Hell Unltd* made by Helen Biggar and Norman Mclaren, with Glasgow Film Theatre. Kim was recently the sound designer for the award-winning *Faslane* by Jenna Watt and composer / performer for Julia Taudevin's *Blow Off.*

www.kimikomoore.com

Louise Stephens (dramaturg)

Louise Stephens is a script reader and dramaturg. She has worked with the National Theatre of Scotland; Tron Theatre; Tiata Fahodzi; Òran Mór (A Play, a Pie and a Pint); Derby Theatre; Curve, Leicester; Live! Theatre; Rifco, and the Playwrights' Studio, Scotland. She often works with maker/performers to help them achieve their goals for performance, most recently working with Rachael Young (*I, Myself and Me*) and Jenna Watt (Flâneurs: Fringe First 2012; Faslane, Fringe First 2016). She was the Literary Officer at the Traverse Theatre and is currently the Deputy Literary Manager of the Royal Court Theatre.

Callum Smith (producer)

Callum Smith is a theatre producer based in Glasgow. He has produced work for companies and artists including Jenna Watt, Sam Rowe, Phoebe Eclair-Powell, Sleeping Warrior Theatre Company, New Room Theatre, Theatre Gu Leòr, Plutôt La Vie and Strange Theatre. He has also worked for some of the UK's most prestigious companies including the National Theatre of Scotland, Tron Theatre and London's Royal Court Theatre, where he was international administrator and project managed the theatre's activity all over the world.

www.callum-smith.co.uk

Text in double quotations indicates verbatim.

I'm standing here, not as a member of this or
that political party, nation, continent, or creed,
but as a human being, member of the species
Man, whose continued existence is in doubt. The
world is full of conflicts; and overshadowing all
these conflicts, is the titanic struggle between the
human race and nuclear weapons.

Almost everybody who is politically conscious
has strong feelings about this issue; but I want us,
if we can, to set aside such feelings and consider
ourselves only as members of a biological species
which has had a remarkable history, and whose
disappearance none of us can desire.

Here, then, is the problem I present to you, stark
and dreadful and inescapable:

Shall we allow nuclear weapons to put an end to
the human race; or the human race to put an end
to nuclear weapons?

I appeal as a human being to human beings:
remember your humanity and forget the rest.

WHERE I STOOD

I didn't write that bit at the beginning, Einstein did. It's a quote from Einstein and Bertrand's manifesto, that they wrote sixty years ago, asking the world leaders not to proliferate the use of nuclear weapons.

I want to be transparent.

It's important that you know what I'm saying.

And what other people are saying.

It's important to hear those other opinions.

To accept that there are other views and experiences.

It's important to say that I'm not here to confirm your pro- or anti-Trident views.

This isn't a friendly guide to the debate. I'm not going to explain everything.

Although I can convincingly argue both pro- and anti-Trident views.

And if, after this, you still want that, then you can buy me a green tea in the bar afterwards.

(beat)

Two years ago, it was a pre-independence referendum Scotland, Alex Salmond was first minister for Scotland, Ed Miliband was Labour leader, David Cameron; Prime Minister, there were six SNP MPs in Westminster. The Paris attacks hadn't happened yet, or the beach shooting in Tunisia but Fukushima had. Trump wasn't president, Britain was still a permanent member of the EU and, spoiler; the House of Commons hadn't yet voted to renew Trident.

Both Yes and No campaigns were using Trident to fan political fervour, one camp demanding that Trident be removed from Scotland, the other warning that defence was not a devolved power and thousands of jobs would be lost at Faslane.

Two years ago, I knew how I felt about Scottish Independence, but I didn't know how I felt about Trident, and I really should have because my family have worked in Faslane with Trident my entire life.

The thousands of jobs that would be lost, that was my family they were referring to, and not some distant family, but the aunties and uncles and cousins that I grew up with. Two years ago, I couldn't tell you what my family actually did in Faslane, we had never talked about it, even though Trident was a huge part of our lives, in every sense. It was like a distant cousin that I'd heard of but hadn't met yet, an estranged member of the family, but with the capability to destroy mankind.

My family agreed to talk to me about Trident, about Faslane and take me into the base. They've also allowed me to use their real names today but I've chosen not to.

I'm very protective of my family.

(beat)

Now, I've discovered there are two kinds of people in the world.

Jenna brings out the CND pin and talks to the audience.

Hands up who here was born in or after 1983?

Picks an audience member with their hand up, and asks;

What does this symbol mean to you?

Audience member answers something like 'Peace Symbol' or 'Mercedes'.

Thank you.

And who here was born in or before 1982?

Picks an audience member with their hand up, and asks;

What does this symbol mean to you?

Audience member usually answers 'CND symbol'

Thank you.

To me.

This is the Peace Symbol.

It's synonymous with the peace movement
during the Vietnam war.

It's synonymous with, for lack of a better term;
hippies.

It's an iconic symbol that transcends language
and class through the generations.

Except it doesn't.

Because this is actually the symbol of the CND;
the Campaign for Nuclear Disarmament.

I didn't know that.

It was designed by Gerald Holtom in 1958.

I didn't know that.

It's semaphore for N *(shows 'N' in semaphore)* and
D *(shows 'D' in semaphore)* Nuclear Disarmament.

I didn't know that.

It was adopted by the peace movement.

I didn't know that.

How did I not know this?

I'll tell you.

This symbol has been culturally reappropriated for my generation.

Anyone a little older than me, usually about seven years older, recognises this as the CND symbol.

Anyone my age and younger tends to initially identify it as the Peace Symbol.

So here we have a generational and cultural gap and I've fallen right through it.

How?

Forrest Gump and Geri Halliwell

Forrest Gump; released in 1994.

Tom Hanks, box of chocolates, Jenny.

Scene; Forrest is standing on a demo platform at the Washington Monument about to speak to the anti-war campaigners during the Vietnam War.

He starts to speak and you hear a little voice
from the crowd shouting his name, it's Jenny,
who he has a deep, deep love for but she keeps
disappearing off with other men who become
increasing violent towards her as the film
progresses. And it's only after Forrest returns
from the Vietnam war that she finds him
remotely attractive. Anyway, they start making
their way towards each other through the crowd.
They struggle through limbless ex-veterans and
hippies, eventually wading into the reflecting
pool and into a beautiful embrace surrounded by
flags and placards with this symbol.

Peace Symbol. Vietnam War. Forrest Gump.

Gerry Halliwell, Spice Girls, Ginger Spice.

In 1997 she performed at the Brit awards with the
Spice Girls. Now what she was wearing for the
performance made headline news; it was a short
body con dress, with a Union Jack on the front,
and, what the media described as 'the Peace
Symbol' on the back.

And that's it, for the next twenty years I
unquestioningly associate this symbol with the
anti-war peace movement, Forrest Gump, and
Geri Halliwell.

Nobody told me that this was the symbol of the
CND, my mum and dad probably assumed that
I knew that.

Or that I wasn't interested in knowing.

And I never asked.

So it wasn't that this information was being withheld from me.

It's that I didn't know it was something I should know.

It wasn't a known unknown.

It was an unknown unknown.

Like the Protect and Survive campaigns, never saw them.

The four minute warning system, couldn't tell you about it.

Russia always being the bad guy, xenophobic movie trope.

And I was only six when the Cold War ended.

Nuclear war was science fiction to me. Imagine that, nuclear war being science fiction.

And that's because for me, growing up when I did, nuclear war never a tangible threat and whether I like it or not, Trident's a part of that.

THE REST

Sound montage of politicians, scientists and philosophers talking about opposing sides of the nuclear debate including; David Cameron, Jeremy Corbyn, Theresa May, Nicola Sturgeon, Mhari Black, Bertrand Russell and Noam Chomsky.

FASLANE BASE

Summer 2015.

I'm standing in Her Majesty's Naval Base Clyde, Faslane.

I'm standing on the West Coast of Scotland on the edge of the Gare Loch. I'm standing twelve miles west of Helensburgh.

And thirty-four miles west of Glasgow.

I'm standing yards away from the UK's nuclear deterrent: Trident. The Trident nuclear weapons system;

Three Vanguard Class Submarines due for renewal and two new Astute Class Submarines Each Trident Submarine can carry sixteen Trident missiles with twelve warheads per missile. The missiles, for the sake of transparency, are actually stored around the coast in Coulport.

In a mountain.

This isn't top secret information by the way, it's all on the MOD website, and you can Google Earth Faslane.

Faslane is strategically placed between Washington and Moscow.

Faslane is strategically placed on a deep sea loch with quick access to the open sea.

Faslane is the only naval base in the UK with the capability to lift subs out of the water.

Faslane utilised the highly skilled engineers being made redundant from the Clyde shipbuilders.

(beat)

Faslane's mesh fences are tall and silver, and topped with razor wire, which curls like icing on a cake. A big naval base cake, with a nuclear submarine filling.

At the South Gate are the naval officer's accommodation and amenities.

And the North Gate is the business end of the base, with the docks and the Shed.

The Shed is enormous and grey and it's where the subs are lifted out of the water for essential maintenance.

David, my cousin got me clearance to be here today.

And it feels exciting, not many people can say they've been in a nuclear naval base.

I made sure to visit the base before I did anything else; visit the Peace Camp, write a freedom of information request or take part in any activism.

Because I knew this avenue would be closed to me once I did those things.

At the North Gate, I'm greeted by an MOD police officer carrying his Heckler and Koch firearm. Not something you see a lot in the UK.

But here, it's strangely reassuring.

David takes me to a porta-cabin for my security briefing. A video.

"No photography or recording equipment permitted." That's annoying. I seriously consider ignoring this.

But I don't, I play the game. David would be in trouble if I didn't. I hear a run down of the different alarms, and what they mean. I get my photo taken.

There's a sign with the base's alert status:
HIGHEST.

I'm given a green pass.

Which means access accompanied anywhere
except the nuke side of the base. Craig, my uncle,
works on the nuke side of the base with the
Trident subs.

My uncle and I haven't seen or spoken to each
other for twenty years. That's not relevant to this
story, it's just a bit of background information.

(beat)

Few people are allowed access to the nuke side
during high alert. Peace campers got over the
fence days before using an old rug.

And William McNeilly the whistle blower
released his Wikileaks document three weeks
before.

(beat)

David takes me to an office overlooking the Loch
to meet his colleagues.

They were all navy submariners but now work in
the base for Babcock not the MOD. Babcock is
the main services contractor.

Not popular.

I ask David's colleagues; what is it you do?

"We make sure everything that goes on a sub is faultless and reliable. The fittings, the fixtures, the nuts, the bolts."

They take pride in their work.

They tell me hand on heart,

"No sub leaves the base unsafe. We're not sending Trident out to war. We're sending our friends, colleagues and family out to sea."

I ask; why do we need Trident?

"Trident protects us."

Okay.

"The US need us to have Trident."

I didn't know that.

"Trident gives a seat at the table."

(to audience) What table?

What do you think of the peace camp?

"I don't agree with them but."

"They're exercising their democratic right."

"They're helpful, they point out the weaknesses in security."

I ask if they've read the whistleblower McNeilly's Wikileaks report?

"Aye, it's anecdotal, McNeilly never experienced half of what he said."

"It feels like a betrayal, you have to be able to trust your colleagues."

"He was very junior. Easy to dismiss."

Do you think we should have nuclear weapons?

"Aye."

"I don't think about it."

"This is my job, I don't have an opinion."

(beat)

David takes me to the waterside.

We walk between tall grey buildings, and along little streets, it's all concrete and steel.

He takes me to the nuke side fence.

It's all that stands between me and the Trident subs.

And there she is.

In the dock.

Trident.

This is the first time I've seen her.

And I'm in awe.

She's enormous, dark and mysterious.

A leviathan.

A shark.

There she sits, quietly, visible, vulnerable.

(beat)

> I visited the base because I wanted to look in the eyes of the people that maintain the UK's nuclear arsenal, I wanted to understand what goes through their minds when they're sending the Trident nuclear weapon system out to sea; and it's not war, or the benefits of British imperialism, it's family.

And those workers are more impacted by the implications of the Trident renewal everyday than we ever are. I've allowed myself to be reassured by David and his colleagues, and after we've talked, I feel like I can accept Trident.

PRO VS ANTI

(to audience)

We all have those little conflicting voices in our heads, and when we have strong opinions about something; it's not that all those other voices go away, it's that that one voice becomes louder than the rest.

We as a group of people, with our views and experiences, we all contain the complexity of this debate and I'm going to hijack that complexity for a moment, and you're going to be all the voices that have been in my head for the last two years.

Jenna moves into the audience with a mic and shifts between the pro- and anti-Trident arguments.

Trident protects us, it's our insurance policy, it protects the UK from being attacked by the likes of Russia, North Korea and China. Russia currently has the largest nuclear arsenal in the world and more importantly the ability to deploy those weapons.

But the Cold War ended twenty-five years ago,
it's 2016 and Trident can't be used to defend
the UK against today's terrorist organisations.
It couldn't be used in retaliation after the
beach shooting in Tunisia, or the Paris attacks,
because today's terrorists are different groups of
people, with different ideologies, that are spread
throughout the world.

Okay but Trident upholds our 'special
relationship' or nuclear alliance with the biggest
power in the world; the US, and Trident is
what makes us a valuable and important ally, it
guarantees us a seat at the table.

(asks audience member) What table?

The table of global affairs. Where decisions are
made.

Right, yeah, that's important.

FASLANE PEACE CAMP

Summer 2015.

I'm standing outside the Faslane Peace Camp.

It's situated on a small strip of common land
which you pass as you drive to Faslane's North
Gate.

The camp is surrounded by MOD owned land and their comings and goings are heavily monitored.

So my being here has registered on a system somewhere, as well as the registration of my mum's car.

It's their thirty-third birthday weekend and the weather's shit.

This is my first time at the Peace Camp though I've passed it many times over the years.

(beat)

This is the point where I should probably admit to you that I have a terrible prejudice.

I'm not sure exactly where it comes from and I'm hugely embarrassed by it.

But I have a prejudice towards: Hippies.

If I had to guess, I'd say it's because since I was little, I've always understood the Peace Camp and its occupants to be in opposition to my family; to the Base.

Anyway, I acknowledge this prejudice now and do what I can to overcome it.

Like force myself to enjoy green tea.

Look, I'm just telling you this so you understand how anxious I am at the thought of entering the Peace Camp.

I'm standing outside the Faslane Peace Camp.

I'm feeling very accepting of Trident so this feels like a hot mess of betrayal.

But I want to hear from this side of the debate.

I want to be convinced that I'm wrong.

And if you want to get the essential anti-Trident rhetoric

The Faslane Peace Camp is the place to go.

I'm met by Andy, not his real name.

He's immediately polite and friendly, and postpones whatever task he was doing to show me around the camp.

He offers me green tea; I politely decline.

The camp is a collection of brightly coloured camper vans and buses, painted with the Peace Symbol / CND symbol and anti-Trident slogans. They've all been converted into communal amenities and shared sleeping spaces with wooden bunks.

Andy proudly shows me the camp's bath which has hot water, before admitting he doesn't really use it.

I laugh gently at the hippie stereotype he's conforming to.

We walk as we talk, and he tells me about life in the camp, the chores, the rules, the alcohol ban.

We pass an enormous banner that says 'Cameron is a pure fanny'; you might have seen it, it was popular on social media.

He tells me that the MOD raided the camp that morning, that they regularly remove protest and campaigning paraphernalia that crosses the boundary onto the MOD land.

I notice the council bins and comment on how great it is that the council collect them.

"No," Andy says, "we organise that ourselves".

It's a small point but it's one of great contention for people in the area. A lot of locals feel the camp is scrounging off the local council at a cost to the taxpayer and they really resent them having their bins collected. So they use a private company, and that private company doesn't then deliver that refuse to the MOD in bags marked 'intelligence'.

Or does it? It doesn't.

Or does it? It doesn't.

Or does it? It doesn't.

(beat)

How many people live here?

"Five, full time at the moment."

Much less than I thought.

There's one camper van that I'm not allowed in.

Andy tries to hide why.

But it's because the occupants are having a smoke.

I again laugh gently at the hippie stereotype they're conforming to.

Andy tells me about how the camp's being bugged by the MOD and that they have to talk in code when they're planning any direct action.

I later asked about MOD surveillance in an FOI, but the MOD denied it.

In one word; "no".

I change the subject and ask Andy why he's decided to become a full-time resident at the Faslane Peace Camp?

"I don't want to get into it, personal reasons, y'know?"

(beat)

No Andy, I don't fucking know.

Why would anyone choose to live in the Faslane Peace Camp for personal reasons?

It's wet, dark, freezing cold, no electricity, little privacy, possibly no privacy with the MOD as a neighbour, you have to chop wood to heat your water and cook your food, there's no internet, it's a hard life.

I'm raging.

I want Andy to tell me that he's in the Peace Camp because he sees himself as an anti-nuclear warrior who refuses to participate in a society that's obviously indifferent to the humanitarian atrocity of nuclear war.

I want him to tell me that he's so impassioned by
the anti-nuclear movement that he has no other
choice but to be at the Faslane Peace Camp;
the front line of the nuclear debate, creating
blockades, breaking into the base, that he lives
and breathes anti-nuclear. That he'll do anything
for the cause.

I want him to reminisce about the time he swam
out into the loch up to a Trident submarine doing
manoeuvres, and had to be pulled out the water
by an MOD patrol boat.

But he doesn't.

And it becomes clear to me, that the camp is just
a place that people go when they need to escape.

I walk out of the camp, feeling disappointed,
feeling let down, feeling pro-Trident.

PRO VS ANTI

*Jenna moves into the audience with a mic and shifts between the pro- and
anti-Trident arguments.*

Trident protects us, it's our M.A.D insurance
policy; Mutually Assured Destruction. The UK
maintaining a nuclear arsenal equivalent to
that of, say, Russia, means neither side has any
incentive to initiate conflict.

Or to disarm, and Russia has a nuclear arsenal thirty-three times the size of the UK's. M.A.D is the most absurd military policy in existence, it basically ensures the destruction of the entire human race. It's a humanitarian atrocity on an incomprehensible level.

Trident will never be used. It's a deterrent. No British Prime Minister is going to press that button. Our special relationship means there are international safe guards, a chain of command responsible for those decisions being taken.

The special relationship actually means Washington has the power of veto over our nuclear missiles. We don't have independent control over the Trident Nuclear program, we have operational control. So if we lose our minds and decide to deploy a missile, Washington can stop us. But what if Washington lose their minds?

This is why we need to keep our position at the table of global affairs.

(asks audience member) What table?

The United Nations Security Council... table. Renewing Trident means we remain one of its five permanent members along with France, China, the US and Russia. We have the power to vote on every issue that's brought before the UN for resolution. The UK has the power to vote on the deployment of peace keepers, enforce economic sanctions, arms embargoes, freeze a country's assets and deploy a collective military force.

Attack one attack all. That is so fucked up.

That's actually a NATO principle but; yes, that's the world we live in.

THE SPECTRUM OF ACTIVISM

I didn't like the Peace Camp.

I thought it would make me feel impassioned; inspired; righteous; anti-Trident.

It didn't.

And if i'm going to be totally transparent with you.

Which I want to be.

I feel the Faslane Peace Camp is doing a disservice to the anti-Trident debate.

WHAT!

(beat)

I know; it's a difficult thing to hear and it's an even harder thing to say.

But it's old fashioned. Like Trident; it's a relic, it's a symbol.

The camp's purpose is to fight nuclear war, how are five people supposed to do this as well as maintain the Peace Camp? It's a difficult place to live, the winters are hard, resources are few and making the daily walks along Faslane's mesh fences to hold a vigil and monitor the base from the local view point must get really boring.

I wouldn't do it. I don't do it.

Instead I meet Ava, not her real name.

A friend gives me her details, telling me that Ava lived in the Peace Camp in the late eighties and raised her children there.

He says, "If anyone's going to persuade you of the anti-Trident view, it's Ava."

(beat)

Autumn 2015.

We meet in Edinburgh at the Peace and Justice centre.

She sits stuffing envelopes with the latest news on Trident and the upcoming anti-Trident demo in London.

I introduce myself and we begin to talk. I have a list of questions for Ava, but instead I put them away and just listen.

Ava tells me about the day she stood on Helensburgh pier watching Trident come up the Clyde, arriving in Scotland for the first time.

She tells me; "It was never supposed to take this long"

That; "Trident was supposed to be gone by now."

That "Trident was never supposed to arrive."

She talks about how she's given up her life for this cause.

The anti-nuclear cause.

She talks about how she didn't plan to raise her children in the Peace Camp.

How she didn't want her son arrested at the age of fifteen for protesting Trident; "He should never have had to do that."

She takes it personally, she's very protective of
her family.

I ask her why she's anti-nuclear.

"Nuclear war is inhumane."

"It's the most horrific thing we can possibly do to
other human beings. I can't accept that there's no
alternative."

"I can't accept that having nuclear weapons is
normal."

I ask her why she's done this for the last thirty
years.

"I have to, if I don't, who will?"

I'm in awe.

(beat)

I tell her about my experience at the Peace
Camp. How I was terrified of going in.

That I was disappointed. That I felt it was
ineffective

And saying all this feels like a huge betrayal.

A betrayal of the left wing liberalist beliefs that I think I hold. Ava asks if I'm "going to go to the anti-Trident demo in London?"

Yeah, maybe. *(adamantly shakes head)*

What I don't admit to Ava is that I'm an imposter. I've never taken part in any activism.

(aside) Well that's not entirely true, I did take part in Bob Geldof's Make Poverty History march. But we all know that doesn't count.

I've never taken part in any real activism.

And that's because I'm a coward, I'm indifferent, I'm afraid. Afraid of being arrested.

Of being caught up in protest violence.

Of being kettled.

Of being a bystander while someone gets beaten by the police.

Of having my name on a list somewhere.

Of being monitored and watched.

Of being other.

Ava says; "Well it's not for everyone, the Peace Camp"

"There's a spectrum of activism."

"For some it's living in the Peace Camp and for others it's stuffing envelopes."

(beat)

I understand now, why Andy wasn't on message and declaring his principles.

I wasn't in the Peace Camp representing the press, or military, or local council.

I was just a human being talking to another human being.

And Andy choosing to live in the Peace Camp for "personal reasons, y'know" wasn't a betrayal of his beliefs or the anti-nuclear cause.

It was a slight against my pre-determined idea of what a peace camper should be.

And it's an indication of a much wider issue;

Not everyone has a choice about where they live, "y'know."

I thank Ava and I'm just about to leave when she calls out "hang on" and hands me a flyer for the anti-Trident Demo.

Thank you, I say, knowing I'll never go.

DIFFICULT TO COMPREHEND

The most difficult thing throughout this journey has been trying to comprehend the enormity of this debate and gain a perceptual understanding of its consequences.

Like every human being I have my cognitive limitations, meaning that even if I know that Trident is a weapon of mass destruction and a humanitarian atrocity, I still can't perceptually comprehend what that means.

Like when scientists or philosophers talk about the power of nuclear weapons they talk about it in terms of 'a Hiroshima'. They reduce the enormous destruction and horror of what happened in Hiroshima to a single unit of measurement, to help us comprehend the impact of a nuclear warhead.

A unit of horror.

So, one Trident warhead has a yield capability of eight Hiroshimas.

But I have no idea what 'a Hiroshima' is.

I know what Hiroshima is, I know that happened there, but I don't know what 'a Hiroshima' feels like, I can't perceptually conceive of it

I can't even imagine what a thousand bodies look like.

So I certainly don't know what it feels like to see forty thousand people killed by a six thousand degree celsius thermal blast so intense that it vapourises their bodies instantly.

Or to be consumed by a firestorm and incinerated before you even know what's happened.

Or to be instantly blinded by the flash and feel your skin instantaneously blister and begin to melt.

I don't know what it feels like. I wasn't there. I can't comprehend it.

And this frustrates me, because is isn't just percent yields, it's people, it's human beings, it's family.

This is what Einstein and Bertrand were talking about when they were pleading with world leaders.

PRO VS ANTI

Jenna moves into the audience with a mic and shifts between the pro- and anti-Trident arguments.

Trident protects us, the renewal of Trident is
our insurance policy against the risks that there
are in our world; a world where we need strong
defences, that protect us from nuclear blackmail,
to ensure our future prosperity.

World powers exist without nuclear weapons;
Spain, Canada, Australia; all signatories of the
NPT agreement, the Non Proliferation Treaty,
which in 1968, the UK signed and agreed to
work toward the cessation of nuclear weapons.
The renewal of Trident breaks this treaty.

Trident's renewal is the maintenance of our
current nuclear arsenal, not the proliferation
of them. We must remain on the UN Security
Council.

Today's prominent philosophers believe that
we could still be a permanent member of the
UN Security Council if we got rid of Trident.
We could be an example for the other nuclear
weapon states to follow.

Unilateral disarmament is not an option,
especially now that we're leaving the EU.

Okay, then. How about this. The UK Trident nuclear weapons program is illegal. It contravenes the Geneva Convention that makes it illegal to deploy an indiscriminate weapon of mass destruction that results in the death of civilians.

(asks audience member) And who has the authority to enforce the Geneva Convention?

The UN Security Council.

FUUUUUUUUUCK

TWENTY YEARS

Spring 2016.

I'm standing in the front room of my uncle's house. We're both twenty years older than when we last spoke.

I never thought at the beginning of this process that Trident would bring me here.

I'm glad it has but this feels like more of a betrayal than anything else I've done in this process. I know my family wouldn't have a problem with me being here.

It just reminds me that I didn't have a choice about my uncle. I was given a side to be on.

And it wasn't his.

And it's taken me this long to come here and that makes me feel shit. But I'm here now.

I meet his new family. They've heard a lot about me. I know nothing about them.

I never asked.

My uncle has a son and fosters children. I didn't know that.

They've just received a baby girl and a three-year-old boy. Michael; not his real name.

She's precious and he's curious.

It's Easter, so I've brought them chocolate eggs.

(Makes 'shit magic trick' gesture)

And I do this shit trick where I hide an egg in each hand and ask Michael to pick one. He doesn't want to.

He thinks this is going to end badly.

But of course it won't, I have an egg in each hand.

But Michael doesn't know that. This is an unknown unknown. Michael eventually picks a hand and is understandably in awe.

And for the rest of the visit I'm the woman who produces eggs from her hands. I ask my uncle how long he'll have Michael.

"The social services always say it'll be a long time, months, years. But we've learned not to listen to them anymore."

"And to take it day-by-day."

"Make sure the kids are healthy and happy and safe one day at a time."

I don't know if I could do that. Let him go at a moment's notice.

I've only just met Michael and I instinctively want to protect him, fix him, undo the damage that's been done to him.

At least I know, here, he's in safe hands. Those hands always made me feel safe.

(beat)

My uncle brings up Faslane first, saying; "I thought that's why you might be here"

I'm embarrassed, it's not the only reason I'm here.

He's signed the Official Secrets Acts, so we can only talk about the known knowns and the known unknowns.

And I don't push him on anything. I'm very protective of my family. I ask him; what's your job at the base?

The information he gives me is too specific, it will identify him. I'm redacting it.

(makes a 'redacted' gesture)

Redacted.

Why do you work at the base?

"It's given me a lot of training opportunities, a lot of qualifications I wouldn't normally get. A pension."

Do you think we need Trident?

"Yes."

Why?

"There are too many threats out there."

What, like terrorists?

"Yeah."

And there's a moment where I can see neither of us believe that.

What do you think about the Peace Camp?

"They're doing a job, like me. They're expressing their views."

Which is?

"They don't think nuclear weapons should exist."

Do you?

"I think we need them. While everyone else has them."

I don't bring up the NPT agreement or the UN Security Council.

Did the base influence your independence referendum vote?

(makes 'redacted' gesture)

Have you ever been exposed to radiation?

"Yeah."

Nuclear radiation?

"Yeah."

When?

"A few times, it's not been serious."

Okay.

"I'm exposed to radiation everyday in my job."

Everyday?

"It's low level. It's harmless, It's normal."

Don't you think that's risky?

"It's my job."

(beat)

He asks if I want to know more.

I don't.

I choose not to ask whether he knows the long-term effects on the body of being exposed to radiation.

I choose not to ask whether he considers the
humanitarian impact of what he does for a job.

(beat)

"It's my job."

That's the answer my family gave me whenever I
asked them what they think about Trident.

"It's my job" feels like the new family fucking
motto.

If my family can't give me an opinion.

Then who's going to persuade me and tell me
where to stand?

(beat)

*Jenna sits back in her uncle's house and repeats the
gesture of the shit magic trick.*

My uncle's just a guy, a guy who happens to
work in a nuclear naval base.

He doesn't have a duty to give me a convincing
argument for being pro-Trident.

My family doesn't have a duty to offer me an
opinion because I haven't bothered to develop

my own. They're normal people with families and personal reasons and something to protect.

They don't present a polarized view of the debate, they present the complexity of it. And they're not telling me what to think or trying to contradict what I already believe.

They want me to have my own opinion, even if it's different from theirs, we'll still be family.

It's time I decide where I stand.

(beat)

CND MARCH

Spring 2016.

I'm standing in the middle of the biggest anti-Trident demo that London has seen in a generation. And I'm not afraid.

I have a placard. Bold. Uncomplicated. No Trident.

I don't like the others. NHS not Trident. Books not Trident. Jobs not Trident.

The reinvestment of the MOD budget is an argument from the anti-Trident side that really winds me up.

Anyone that works with a budget, knows you
can't just take money from one pot and put
it in another, and the MOD budget has been
protected from austerity cuts, meaning, the
billions we don't invest in Trident will be invested
in arms used everyday to kill civilians.

(beat)

There are cries of;

"We say welfare, you say warfare!"

And

"Bairns not bombs!"

But I don't chant, I can't, I don't want to.

The pro- and anti-factions make me feel like I
stand with them or against them.

And that's not true.

The debate isn't binary, it's a spectrum. I
understand that now.

And at the march I can truly see the complexity
of it.

(beat)

Trafalgar Square is packed.

This is what thousands of bodies looks like.

Each bringing their own views and experiences
to the march.

I needed to be here because whatever I feel
about Trident, it's in the hands of a government
and a Prime Minister that I don't trust.

And while it exists; I know that Ava will commit
another thirty years of her life to the anti-nuclear
cause. To protect us.

And my family will continue to make Trident as
safe as they can. To protect us.

Because I have no choice but to live in a world of
nuclear weapons.

My only choice is whether I live with the
awareness, or not, of what nuclear weapons exist
to do.

(beat)

I'm standing on the ledge of one of the fountains.
I don't particularly enjoy being in large crowds.

I'm surrounded by octogenarian CND couples
and their families and I ready myself to give up
my ledge at any moment.

I stand waiting for the speakers as the square
begins to swell with people. I look up towards the
gallery and the bodies merge into a hot mess.

But then there's a sudden movement in the
crowd. Bodies pull away aggressively from the
gallery.

Screaming starts, at first; yells of confusion that
turn quickly into screams of terrible pain. The
crowd surges and bodies start to fall over the
balcony crushing the people below.

I'm pulled off the ledge of the fountain as people
scream and throw themselves into the water.

Everything goes dark as bodies stand on me,
on my muscles and limbs and hair, trying to get
into the fountain. They're screaming, they're all
screaming.

A wave of heat blasts over my body and I
scrunch up my face against the force of it. I smell
my burnt hair and flesh before I feel it.

I can't open my eyes, they're searing.

All I can see is red.

All I feel is fire.

I grasp out around me, trying to find the fountain.
I feel a shape, and I stretch my arm across it. It's
sticky and burning hot.

I gasp for breath and force my eyes open.

A woman's charred body, flesh black is cracked
and fizzling. The skin on her arms comes away in
my fingertips.

My hands are swollen and bloodied and
blistered.

Traumatized bodies walk around with their skin
hanging like ribbons, trailing through the ash,
and the grit and glass.

Bodies broken, battered, buried under the weight
of each other.

Incinerated bodies in contorted positions, mouths
open silently screaming.

Fountains full of lifeless bodies, face down with
their flesh still searing.

And through the haze of heat and horror; Ava
appears.

I can't believe it, I see Ava.

She's stepping over and through the bodies and rubble handing out flyers. I catch her eye.

Ava!

She looks at me.

It's Jenna, we met at the Peace and Justice Centre. I decided to come.

She smiles and hands me a flyer, like a baton.

A torch.

A cause to carry for another thirty years.

(Jenna pulls the CND pin out of her pocket and looks at it in the palm of her hand, she looks up.)

Black

WWW.OBERONBOOKS.COM

.